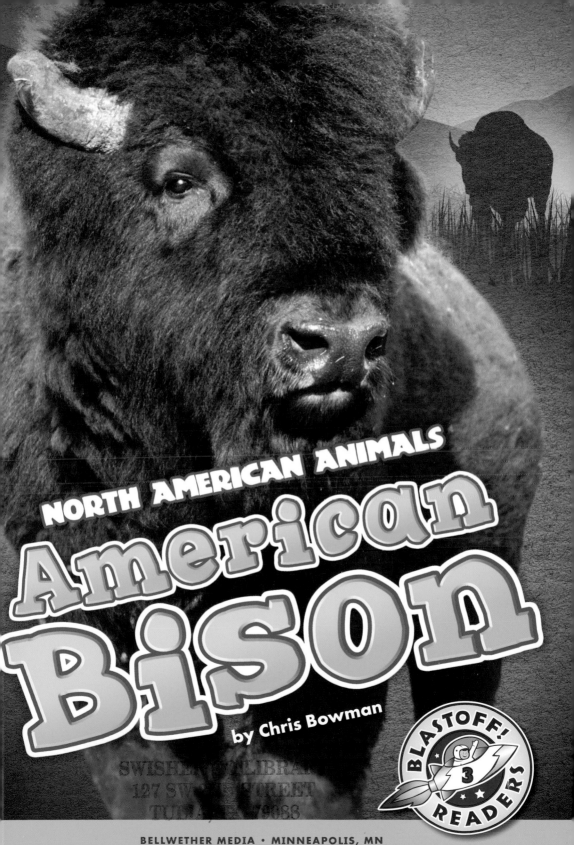

NORTH AMERICAN ANIMALS

American Bison

by Chris Bowman

BLASTOFF! READERS
3

BELLWETHER MEDIA • MINNEAPOLIS, MN

Note to Librarians, Teachers, and Parents:

Blastoff! Readers are carefully developed by literacy experts and combine standards-based content with developmentally appropriate text.

Level 1 provides the most support through repetition of high-frequency words, light text, predictable sentence patterns, and strong visual support.

Level 2 offers early readers a bit more challenge through varied simple sentences, increased text load, and less repetition of high-frequency words.

Level 3 advances early-fluent readers toward fluency through increased text and concept load, less reliance on visuals, longer sentences, and more literary language.

Level 4 builds reading stamina by providing more text per page, increased use of punctuation, greater variation in sentence patterns, and increasingly challenging vocabulary.

Level 5 encourages children to move from "learning to read" to "reading to learn" by providing even more text, varied writing styles, and less familiar topics.

Whichever book is right for your reader, Blastoff! Readers are the perfect books to build confidence and encourage a love of reading that will last a lifetime!

This edition first published in 2015 by Bellwether Media, Inc.

No part of this publication may be reproduced in whole or in part without written permission of the publisher. For information regarding permission, write to Bellwether Media, Inc., Attention: Permissions Department, 5357 Penn Avenue South, Minneapolis, MN 55419.

Library of Congress Cataloging-in-Publication Data

Bowman, Chris, 1990- author.
 American Bison / by Chris Bowman.
  pages cm. – (Blastoff! Readers. North American Animals)
 Includes bibliographical references and index.
 Summary: "Simple text and full-color photography introduce beginning readers to American bison. Developed by literacy experts for students in kindergarten through third grade"– Provided by publisher.
 Audience: Ages 5-8.
 Audience: K to grade 3.
 ISBN 978-1-62617-184-8 (hardcover : alk. paper)
 1. American bison–Juvenile literature. I. Title.
 QL737.U53B687 2015
 599.64'3–dc23
                    2014041946

Printed in the United States of America, North Mankato, MN.

Table of Contents

What Are American Bison?

American bison are the largest hoofed **mammals** in North America. They are found only in **protected areas** and national parks.

N
W   E
S

Extinct

Extinct in the Wild

Critically Endangered

Endangered

Vulnerable

Near Threatened

Least Concern

American bison range = ▮

conservation status: near threatened

However, they once roamed prairies and **savannahs** across most of the **continent**.

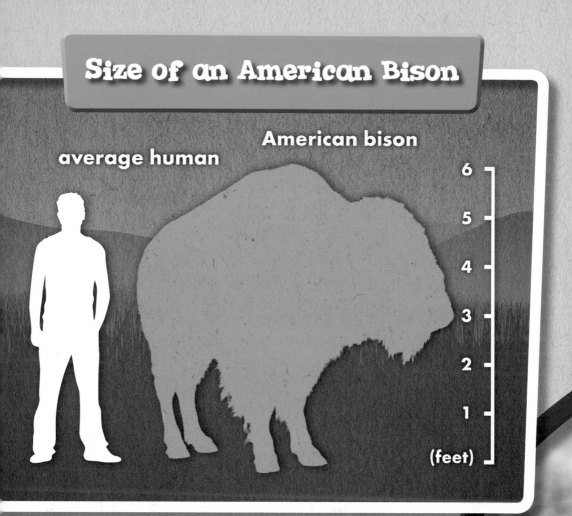

Size of an American Bison

average human

American bison

6
5
4
3
2
1
(feet)

Bison are heavier than North America's other land animals.

Large males can weigh over 2,000 pounds (907 kilograms)! They can stand 6 feet (1.8 meters) tall at the shoulders.

Bison have dark brown coats. Their fur is longer on the front half of their bodies. They grow thick beards.

hump on back   **curved horns**   **shaggy beard**

Curved horns grow out of
their huge heads. Large humps
shape their backs.

9

Wallowing and Grazing

Bison rest during the heat of the day.

Sometimes they **wallow** in dirt. This keeps them cool. It also keeps flies from biting.

They **graze** in the evening and early morning. These **herbivores** eat mostly grasses and **sedges**. In winter, they find twigs and other foods under the snow.

On the Menu

wheat sedge

sagebrush

windmill grass

sand dropseed

blue grama grass

little bluestem

Bison spit up their food. Then they chew it again as **cud**. This helps them break down the plants.

Male bison are called **bulls**. Every summer, bulls compete for females, or **cows**.

They **bellow** and stamp their feet. Sometimes they ram heads and fight with their horns.

In spring, each cow gives birth to one **calf**. The baby can run within three hours of being born! Still, mom keeps her calf close.

Baby Facts

Name for babies:	calves
Size of litter:	1 calf
Length of pregnancy:	9 to 9.5 months
Time spent with mom:	1 year

Mountain lions, wolves, and other **predators** go after babies.

However, they usually stay away from bison **herds**. They do not want to face a **stampede**.

Calves are born red. Within four months, their coats turn brown.

They need special care until age 1. Then they are members of the herd!

Glossary

bellow—to call with a deep sound

bulls—male bison

calf—a baby bison

continent—one of the seven land areas on Earth

cows—female bison

cud—food that has been spit up to be chewed again

graze—to feed on plants in grasslands

herbivores—animals that only eat plants

herds—groups of bison that live and travel together

mammals—warm-blooded animals that have backbones and feed their young milk

predators—animals that hunt other animals for food

protected areas—lands that are kept in a natural state to protect animals and plants

savannahs—grasslands with very few trees

sedges—grassy plants that grow in wet areas

stampede—a herd of animals running together to escape danger

wallow—to roll in the dirt

To Learn More

AT THE LIBRARY
Elston, Heidi M.D. *Buffaloes Eat and Grow.*
Minneapolis, Minn.: Magic Wagon, 2015.

Magby, Meryl. *American Bison.* New York, N.Y.:
PowerKids Press, 2012.

Potts, Steve. *American Bison.* Mankato, Minn.:
Capstone Press, 2012.

ON THE WEB
Learning more about American bison
is as easy as 1, 2, 3.

1. Go to www.factsurfer.com.

2. Enter "American bison" into the search box.

3. Click the "Surf" button and you will see a
   list of related web sites.

With factsurfer.com, finding more
information is just a click away.

Index

The images in this book are reproduced through the courtesy of: F1 Online/ SuperStock, front cover; visceralimage, pp. 4-5; Volodymyr Burdiak, pp. 6-7, 9 (top left), 14; Leigh Trail, p. 8; Nagel Photography, p. 9 (top center); BGSmith, p. 9 (top right); Eric Isselee, p. 9 (bottom); Jim Parkin, p. 10; westernphotographs, p. 11; Eduard Kyslynskyy, pp. 12-13; USDA-NRCS Plants Database, p. 13 (top left); SeDmi, p. 13 (top right); SirinS, p. 13 (center left); Matt Lavin/ Flickr, p. 13 (center right); Bildagentur Zoonar GmbH, p. 13 (bottom left); Chhe/ Wikipedia, p. 13 (bottom right); Thomas Groberg, pp. 14-15, 17; Darren Baker, pp. 16-17; Geoffrey Kuchera, pp. 18-19; Donald M. Jones/ Corbis, p. 20; Arco/ C. Hutter/ Glow Images, p. 21.